Pan: the Trickster

in poetry and life

Pan: the Trickster
in poetry and life

Maryann Schacht

McCaa Books • Santa Rosa

McCaa Books
1604 Deer Run
Santa Rosa, CA 95405-7535

ISBN 978-0-9838892-8-1

First published in 2013 by McCaa Books,
an imprint of McCaa Publications.

Printed in the United States of America
Set in Minion Pro

Pan illustrations by Kathy Hainke.

www.mccaabooks.com

For Morris who accepts that "What is-is what it is."

CONTENTS

Observations

PASSAGES

*Beloved Pan: give me beauty in the inward soul
and may the outward and inner man be at one*

Plato's *dialogues*

Pan's Path

Beware--all humans encounter
the path of Pan
The God Pan loves seduction
He hides in the green of unknowing

He fillets dreams, inspires,
schemes, invites you to fence
with deduction
Pan's way is never linear

Trilling flute notes he promotes
the desire for perfection
then he sets a trap
in a labyrinth of distraction

He may cause you to stumble
and scrape your knees
heat up your passion
freeze words on your tongue

He beckons the chef to over season
or under cook while discovering
new combinations,
then laughs at each disaster

Pan tricks you along
the path to advancement
for in error he lays the lesson
Believe it or not with every step

Pan is the leaven of poets
Pan is the master of dance

The Spanish Dining Table

When I creep beneath the table, the Spanish dining table,
I feel its iron braces and trace its wood design and marvel
at how smooth it is, how dark it is. This cave is mine.
In this place I make a me, a gypsy me who laughs and
bangs a tambourine. I read the future in my palms and
know that I can disappear.

Ssh Gypsy. Ssh Gypsy.

Peeking through the table lace l see no feet but understand
that overhead are fingerbowls
and china cups just waiting for grownups to appear.
If I make noise, I'll give away my hiding place.

Ssh Gypsy. Ssh Gypsy.

Cast your mandala on the ground soundlessly then vanish.
Now I'll turn into a gypsy moth and flutter here beneath
the linen cloth.
How soft I am. How small I am. I will not fear.

No one will ever know that I am hiding here.

When I was a child I read

"When I was sick and lay a-bed,
I had two pillows at my head,
And all my toys beside me lay,
To keep me happy all the day."

—Robert Lewis Stevenson: *The Land of Counterpane*

My ears still hurt but

I imagine the soldiers and I forget.

I send my pain to the battlefield

where bravery will never yield.

Before my eyes the soldiers drill

and illness vanishes – vanquished

I think of that poem many times.

I love the thought. I love the rhyme.

It's served me well throughout my years.

It dries my tears

whenever life throws me a curve.

I have that small poem in reserve.

It is engrained in memory.

Words do have power over pain.

After the prom

I swim hard

Lake water slips
soft satin
over naked limbs
I belong in liquid

It eases hurt
nothing measured
nothing said
He doesn't care

I am aware
I can't recover me
at least the Me
I was

The me I thought I knew
has been ejected
displaced from
amniotic innocence

Who am I now?
No jellyfish
to be erased
I will still swim

With steady strokes
cutting through
the tears in dark
deep water

I swim hard

Recognition

A nightmare stares at me
front face -- head on

A soul mirror
reflecting what
    I insist
    I'm not

A toothsome boar rifling
 the grass snorts
    demanding
    inclusion

This is the hog who
    sears by innuendo
    snorting

plows in a shallow ditch
    urinating on wishes
    craving visibility

He will not be transformed
unless I can agree

This dark shadow
    growling
    grunting

hairy thing is mine
He is part of me

New Decor

The room
where they loved
wall-papered

Shared bed
undone as if
they never were

Packed and crated
Puppets and banjoes
all quieted

Coupled times
decanted
still born

Over

Rain Call

Raindrops push at
the window screen
eye candy
enticing me to view
abstract patterns
tiny lanterns
messengers
of storms to follow

Sycamore leaves
not yet freed
by wind
cling stubbornly
tenaciously to branch
Like me
I do the same
Still, it's time

Body tired, worn
moving slower
dreaming heavy
through the night
Here, then gone
the phantom calls
Winter's here

Generation Bridge

On the close and warm
we place dream pebbles
energized by - polished by - honed by - caring
She shakes her head
astonished by switched on Bach
Impromptu suppers
paper diapers
I watch her stitch
embroidery
and scent her scarf
with dried gardenias
Her silken hand
veined in wisdom
strokes mine
so newly stained in
mother's milk
We bend boundaries
as we walk down
a corridor
on the mosaic floor
of generations
drifting on the close and warm

Soft Whispers

A gentle love is ours, my friend
        Blending
        strength
        supporting

Highs and lows
        in joy and grief
        sustained
        in wavering belief

A gentle love is ours my friend
        Tender
        Easy
        Slender

in every day ineptitudes
        Divided
        striving
        varied moods

A gentle love is ours my friend
        Binding
        kindly
        winding

Through vicissitudes
        shared
        human passions
        attitudes

A gentle love is ours my friend

Now

Day drifts
Sand shifts

Whatever
went before

settles
to particulate

Imperatives
elided

No need for
making beds

cooking dinner
writing

This is our
Now

to breathe
moist air

and savor
the salted

flavor of
I love you

Carried by birds

I often forget that
grass kernels don't require
me to plant their seeds
birds will carry them

nor does grass
need ants crawl
to spread them
There's breeze

Grass needs no extra frills

Butterfly bushes bend
and fan enticing
bees to drink deep
 in late afternoon

Even as tree leaves curl
signaling fall
I can sense
hotness in the air

I relish the warm and one last swim of summer

Season Change

October rain
paints mold spots
on falling pears and grapes
What was green in summer
is spotted brown and worn

Chill whispers a
pine scented aria of
imminent change and pace
Wheat fields are picked and stacked
It's autumn

Geese quicken and
rise in perfect V
exchanging leaders
no strife to be seen
in formation

A table dressed
with fresh washed cloth
has fewer places set
for harvest has faded
to quietude

Moonlit Night

Last night the moon was round and full
a pregnant lady presaging birth
        to thought and poesy

The moon was a lamplight,
a searchlight, a skylight glowing
        I watched her in awe

Set in a silken skein of royal blue
night redolent with cricket calls
        and owl whoops

Summer whispered - Time slowed
I touch my lover's arm, we embrace
        and amble off to bed

But the moon refused to keep
her beams in place, she spilled them
        into dreamtime

murmuring tales of mythic gods
and my miniscule place
        in the cosmos

That moon comprised of dust and storm
is a talisman that whirls in
        permanence of constant change

Flotsam and Jetsam

Kids grown and gone
Time to move on
What passed for flash
is now residue trash
  Flotsam and jetsam

Donate to charity
Never mind parity
Stuff is just stuff
We've had enough
  Flotsam and jetsam

That broken pump
Off to the dump
Neglected and old
Devoured by mold
Definitely
  Flotsam and jetsam

I've a lump in my throat
as I throw out my coat
and that awful wool hat
ripped apart by the cat
The old family life
spreads like spam
on the knife of Remember

Passages

Burnt toast
Overdone roast
Coffeepot drips
Potato chips
Gravy stains
On counterpanes
The painted bird
considered a treasure
The oversized table
we didn't measure
Forgotten objects
Half started projects

Backyard parties and Hawaiian flairs
Faded umbrellas and canvas chairs
Clay garden pots
Other what knots?
Is everything
     Flotsam and jetsam

Letting go the igniter
Moving on traveling lighter
Another inning
A New beginning
No more acquiring
So inspiring saying no to
     Flotsam and jetsam

Pan: the Trickster

Put well used dishes
and ceramic fishes
with last years wishes
in popcorn wrap
the wine glasses
and the vases of grasses
Make spaces if you can
for the shabby afghan
And there may still be room
for one more broom
In the moving crate
Marked special freight

Reserve it
Preserve it
Conserve it

along with the laughs
and Photographs and Paintings
not everything is
      Flotsam and Jetsam

Backpack down

Hummingbird wings
beat inside my head
reminding me of

things to come
things gone by
and worry

useless to grouse or grind teeth
when pitching tents
in a pristine place

Here in the lush of bird calls
memory's
left on office walls.

Squirrels crunch leaves
and the wing beats stop
cell phones silence

in forest air
inhaling sounds of space
and waterfalls

Ancestors whisper
signaling pathways
every day far away

Suspended between before and now
ceding abreaction
reverie becalms

knowing is all in the woodland

St. Genevieve

St. Genevieve, the Saint of light
deserted me last night
I tried to switch a lamp on
it sputtered
leaving dark thought
in its wake
slaking head and heart
in unknowing

I breathe and
count the ins and outs
and hold myself in stillness
This is the time of waiting
seconds before revealing
new direction

These elder years
swell in rearrangement
from splash and spit
from source to sea
life cuts its path and
moves through mud banks
and stone cliffs

Passages

It is in mist
plants set down roots
even the small ones
For everything there is
a time to show and shine
and liquid thread
glows in ocean narrows

Truth waits
to be unveiled beneath
the flight of sparrows

As Years go by

That familiar face is
etched with lines
His back is bent
His walking slowed

We two have shared
the yoke of time
weathered deaths and births
family and friends

We stay paired
tethered in caring
negotiating moods
that fluctuate and irritate

Still, I can see
that sweet soul
the one who joked
and made me laugh

His eyes still shine
with knowing
Just as they did
when he chose me

Duly noted

Lives are marked in photographs of
Children hugging teddy bears
Catching salamanders
Camping out and chattering

Life consists of change

Old videos attest to shouts
and laughs and splashes
in the pool. The days are warm
but now I have no need to swim

My travel days are tucked away
in picture frames and boxes
gathering dust as the clock
ticks and rearranges

From Babe to child to tall to shrink

The humming birds and wrens
whirr about in the garden
Awareness abounds in smaller sounds
after the children move on

The stage is set anew

As memories fade to sepia
adventures retreat to recall
What was buried to be mined
in the landfill of generations

Time numbers the pages

Olding

I've accommodated to being slower
I relish the fact that I no longer vie
to be first or best in my class

I acknowledge I've lived fully
Yes, I've missed a prize or two
But wiser now, naps are welcome

It's when I recognize that I
no longer entertain with ease
It's then I freeze.

What happened to that mind
so filled with good intentions
Is it hiding somewhere

Or simply awaiting new ways
to flash in sunshine.
fast pace slowed down to walker

It's when fatigue embraces me
bed to chair; chair to bed
passion consigned to remembrance

Then I remind myself
I've lived fully
This too will pass

Inheritance

Your voice is mine
Same pitch
Same timbre
Same design

Witch on broom
you push and prod
pick up
all crumbs
with courage

Birds need seeds
to power flight
regret is
senseless
useless

You are alive

Paraphrase

Reframe

Strive

I am your parable

Do you see what I see?

Or is it that we name a thing
and then agree when the
colorblind see green as gray
red is only the top of a traffic light

Some of us see auras
some don't, but energy is there
dark spots in lighted hallways
it's everywhere, it's there

Once I thought the answer lay
in near sightedness
but testing I found common ground
Others see auras too

You may not think what I think
You don't choose the things I love
not furniture or overtures or the
ice cream flavor of the month

I insist on silken sheets
when I know flannel will do fine
while you accept and are content
with either - or, no matter

We are parts of something more
with different aspirations
You wonder at the reach of sky
I, at the grains of beach

We are human
all too human
Separate - in together

It is the Fog

It is the fog that teaches
I'm more than pulse
and body rhythms

I am strong
Foot crunching brush
with cadence

Breathing the crisp
of consciousness
weather on my skin

Climbing is struggle
facing windward
stretching me

It is in challenge
Fear dissipates
Boundaries dissolve

And I relish my inner dark

Pan: the Trickster

Macon: 1883 - 1903

Follow me she declared, "If we are to be paired it will be on shipboard and not before. I'm going to America. I don't care about choopahs or what people say. I need to be free. So? Stay behind if you wish by yourself."

He doesn't wish. Rosie packs up her trousseau of linens and lace, books a passage for two and sails off.

Man and wife they arrive at Castle Rock with brand new names and brand new lives. The settlement workers say, "Make your way to Macon. There's opportunity there." It's a long hard trip, and the train coughs smoke, and the new bride complains, and the new groom nods and keeps reading his book.

In Macon, Georgia, Papa opens a shop, a tailor shop, where he cuts and stitches cravats and coats and his fingers fly and his scissors snip. Finest of style, the patterns well fit, he's a gentlemen's tailor. Southern gentry vie to buy Papa's clothes in Macon.

A tall, straight man, and a blue-eyed man who continues to do as he's always done: work hard, read the bible, and ponder each portion. He's a Jewish scholar that Papa.

Rosie, his wife, loves her new Georgia life: making matzo Brie, baking peaches in pie, laughing and dancing at the immigrant lodge, bossing Papa and friends, setting new trends. She's the Queen of her circle in Macon.

Now and then she takes time to relish escape from the rancor and rape of her Polish hometown Czestochowa. Their houses and shops were raided every so often in the Jewish quarter, her quarter. Life is different here, though leftover fear hangs on the clotheslines in Macon.

Pan: the Trickster

A daughter is born and then a son, every other year another one. Five children born, American born.

Chickens run free 'til their necks are wrung, blessed then undressed by the "schochet." Feathers fly. Flesh is boiled or fried. The challah is braided and left to rise. Friday at sundown candles are lit and the Mama "benches." It's Sabbath.

Black Mammy Ruth comes to care for the youth. She regales them with tales: "Creep up on that hen, watch her close, git her eggs jest as they drop, rub 'em ever so gentle over your eyes and they'll shine and be beautiful." That's how it was in Macon.

Children play hide and seek warning each other not to peek. They climb fences, chase cows, muddy knickers and skirts, and speak with the slow southern twang of the neighborhood gang.

Papa keeps a barrel on the big front porch in which cherries age into wine. It is not to be tasted! But the wine is so sweet it begs to be sampled and slurped, and Essie, the eldest, can't resist. She swipes and dips until her mouth is red with cherry juice.

Brother Michael calls out, "Messy Essie, "There's trouble ahead for sure. A switch is just waiting for you."

"Don't you tell," Essie says, ever so sweetly "That switch isn't for me all alone. If you tell I may catch it for drinking, but you get it too cause you're snitching."

We haven't a 'Minyan' and I know I'm a girl, but we can say Kaddish: the handkerchief's dead. We can bury my mischief no one will know…." Side by side they solemnly swore "Not to tell nobody never." They buried mischief in Macon.

Then the Klan burnt a cross saying, "Strangers beware there's a census coming to Macon.

Haunted by danger and a past of pogroms, they pack up and move north to New York. Mama warns, "Keep still; keep your distance. Don't let anyone know our business. Just play with each other."

She said all of this with insistence.

Mandelbrot, and the coo-coo clock, a fine lace cloth, brought from far away.

Papa wearing lapels of blue satin. Boys sing the Barukot off key while they kick each other under the table so Mama doesn't see.

The family may expand and learn to be wise in American ways. But a faded sepia snap shot shows an immigrant family.

Starting over. Starting over. Starting over.

Customs may alter, but the memories last; in every today there lingers a past.

OBSERVATIONS

Pan is the God of pastures, forest flocks, and herds.
He is nature both raw and beautiful.

K. Hainke

In a world of disarray

Climb hard
the hill is steep

Fear slips her
silken gown
around all senses

Shouldering
machinations

Politics
crowding out daffodils
cracking geodes

The air is thin
and handholds spare

Granite climbs take courage
Clowns and Demagogues
come and go

Shape-shifting
every decade

Pomo Lost

Saltu Hesi (Spirits of Nature)

A Pomo band
Lived on this land
Finding
Winding
Basket reeds
Stringing beads

Merchants
of the Mayacamas range
until the change

When Fur traders
Moved them
Enslaved them
Hooting
Looting
Shooting
For sport

Annihilating
Devastating
A race

The Interface
Of those who want
And those who have
Bad times
Sad times
For the Pomo

Observations

Invaded
Raided
Degraded
Robbed
Raped
Pilloried

Blood spilled
on clay
Resistance
Molded
Enfolded
In bed rock

Once Hunters
now hunted
as prey
they pray
The Sweet grass
stunted

They sang and
they danced
As the settlers advanced

Bole Maru
The Pomo called to
Spirits of nature
And the souls
of dead forebears
Unheard

Pan: the Trickster

Tribe scattered
Discarded
Disregarded

New millers
Grind grain
Milk cows
and settle
Taking pride inside
Pioneering mettle

Covet
Unchecked
Progress to
Regress

Ghosts come unbidden
for hidden
in the marrow
of place

is sorrow
my home is built
on that alloy
and there is sadness
in my joy

Concerto at 7 AM

On the radio this morning
there's music unknown
Composer, place, era
do not matter as
violins, cellos, French horns and
trumpets enter into now
traversing centuries with sound
Who chose those notes?
Was there pain in the creation
or the seeking of acclaim?
Was there no attention paid
to audience applause?
Was it all consuming?
Was the music all?
Could the artist manage a family life?
Was there a lover or a steady wife?
Past desires hint truth on audio wire.
Paths twist and turn, the music burns
through pages of vibrations
Eviscerated egos vanish
as note on note evolves and drops
swirling from coffee cup to
lip and tongue
A musician still delivers
Eternity at breakfast

Diamonds to Coal

Hard times

Rock hard times
the Coal's dirty
    and soft
      it's poisoning
      the water

Daily news bombards us
assaults us
      Paralyzes
      Demoralizes
      Immobilizes

No time for wise ways
to assuage the rage
      Too much hate
      immolates
      an unstable state

Kindness retreats
No one misses a beat
      as the middle class
      shrinks
      in hard times

Observations

Swindlers plead
guilty to greed
　　　Another one's fired
　　　more folks retire
　　　in hard times

Beekeepers strive
to find bees in the hive
　　　After the fact
　　　no second act
　　　in hard times

The question becomes
who's picking the plums
　　　What's helpful
　　　What's hurtful
　　　in hard times

Grit and gravel unravel
as a journeyman pushes
　　　his empty cart
　　　survival's an art
　　　in hard times

What do we know?

Part of my brain calculates
another part moves me to wonder
about the mystical crossing of synapse
and if neurons collapse into chaos

What is it that makes hair grow
or our legs dance to music and song?
Is it by chance or conception
and does it matter at all ?

I marvel at the ways I respond
Is it faith or pheromones?
If I had bone cells implanted
would I still be the am that I am?

Perhaps living's just labels and language

Some people ignore what they see
blind to poverty around them
Others despair when a rabbit has died
and beg for a magical cure

Does DNA govern our lifetime?
Sociology alter its shape?
I can't be alone when I ponder
What's driving pillage and rape

There are villages laying in ruin

Some of us, marvel at being
Is awareness a communal trait?
Does it hide deep in our genomes?
Is it a matter of fancy or fate?

Observations

Native peoples call the forces
in nature to belch fire from
the Earth mother core
Their Heaven's below

If that could be so
is there a which or a why?

Some have grown rich with trophy
others raise chapels and pray
But is the life that we're living a fable?
Perhaps it's a form of pretend

It's by consensus a table's a table

We decide that one color's green
what and which words to consider obscene
But is there really a better or worse?
Perhaps it's all labels and language

Is aversion embedded in style
a choice of passion and drama
Whether it 's mythic or actual fact
all we can be sure of -- is that

We begin
     and we grow
          and we end

Anteus Warning

Without beacons or
bearings we struggle
for power displacing
balance with greed

Once we made tools
out of dawn stones
blessed them, carved
them to art forms

Sidetracked we
chipped and shaped them
from gemstones to
to objects for killing

All but forgotten
the myth of Anteus
who disregarded his ties
to the land

Wrestling ungrounded
Choosing pride over prudence
He was brought
to his knees defeated

Will we do as he did
ignore our natural ties
dishonor spring rain
and renewal

Or can the myth be our guide to remembrance

Parable of Cultivation

An arborist prunes
Slicing limbs the
overgrown unbalanced
Strategically he rips and saws
confident in his knowledge
but a child stands below
wonders at the range of change
That limb was home to blue jays

No safety net for birds
Or for the boy who wanders dreaming
climbing amidst the clamber
It's not the hammer that he fears
Listening for the pulsing calls
He wonders instead
if birds shed tears

The tree is now reshaped
roots descend and reach
deep into earth for nurture
New tender shoots will sprout
as a tree survives its trimming
The child grows to see wasps
and ants as well as honey bees
Life alters contours every day
as an arborist cuts and a boy sows

Repair

There are men on the roof
next door
removing rot
      stripping
      hammering

Stretching sheets
of white plastic
weather proofing
      Proficiently
      Efficiently

I wonder if we
could tile life that way
      avoiding shadow
      avoiding sadness

Oh, if I could roof my brain
to dream a perfect
      seamless dream
      safe and secure

beneath overlapping shakes
there would be
      No cracks
      No leaks

No dampness in the layers

History's Hymn

Screams form soundless
as announcements
address and drone
in constant cacophony
pronouncements pound
hard in a war zone
  Headless
  Needless
  Heedless
Picasso paints true life
not distortion
For the powerful
insist on their portion
Peeing on corpses while
Everyman crawls in disgrace
  Legless
  Wounded
  Sightless
Lead on soldier lead on
to more lust as
your weaponry blasts
Ever faster and surer
erasing the past and the future
young boys are martyred
  Muddied
  Bloodied
  Dead

Wakeup Call

In our age faith versus science
believers state fables with force
ignoring stress on resources
the aquifers are drying

The jet stream snaps at the ice caps
setting bears awash in the sea
tornados chop cities to flatland
typhoons roil ocean and shore

Neo-luddites warn against progress

Insisting cell stems are human - alive
and not to be dissected or studied
That would be a challenge to God
It's better by far to remain as - we are

Research halted - vision muddied

Cover up cancer with sunscreen
Let disease be ordained without cry
as genetically food can be altered
and the shale is fracked for oil

That takes complex understanding

Robber barons ignore facts
or advancement- count coin
as displacement of fear
and a garbage pit grows in the ocean

While coral reefs disappear

Threatened

Gray skies spill down acid rain
The snow packs below normal
And in the chill computers transmit
the news of devastation

Tornadoes wash waste ashore
pouring ocean onto land
We collaborate and blame weather
and another species disappears

Cheering at Olympic games
ignoring murder everywhere
we find pleasure as we play while
the cat naps and the dolphin drifts

Deluded some still dream
that once before machine gun
magazines and drones
life was simple slow and fair

But war and death were always there
We stumble unalarmed distracted
preoccupied by toys and cars
As our world grumbles, on its axis

Shelter

Wrap all my heartbeats
in silk cloth, lace them
with steel thin - threads
Homestead within a cozy hive
then spin untruth to logic

Demand to see and feel
and hear - birdsong forever
I train to keep
the shadows out and will
myself left-brained

If now and then gray film glides in
choking lungs and heart and breath
I face the mist head on
and know it's Death
that hovers by

I gather strength
for one more breath
refuse to dwell in anguish
anxiety must be dispelled
It will not -- cannot languish

All life that's lived is but a pause
The best of hives is trimmed in gauze

Krill in abundance

Flights of seagulls circle above
awaiting their turn in the food chain
An ocean once rich with orcas and fish
once fed on krill in abundance

Now glaciers have calved
spewing ice into water
Tornadoes blow rich soil dry
hurricanes flood over levies
causing whole towns to die

Earth plates are grinding to earthquakes

Olding each day I am weary
from the want to return to what was
There may be a chance to adapt and invent
but lichen and sea shoals are fragile

Listen: the planet is crying

The warming is here
arriving full bore
to challenge our core and our will
and the call to drill ever deep into permafrost

Listen: Mother Gaia is dying

African Aids

Rain

Soggy grain

Mud terrain

Mold

Soured

Raped

Devoured

By dominance

Poverty

Pretense

Overpowered

Deflowered

Overcome

A young girl is crying

Unseen

There are specters everywhere
wisps and wasps airborne
on dreams and daydreams

Enveloped by our busy lives
invention glimmers in minds
souls and blood flows

Slim shards embed Egyptian glass
in ancient statue polish
in utility pots of clay

Reminders from a somewhere else
perhaps a fourth dimension
as real as scent and touch and smell

Elusive rust resides inside us
we wander about in angel dust
eyes closed and hard of hearing

Taps

Oil muddy birds on beaches
my brain slowed at the sight
mixing dates and numbers in heartbeats
Slag coats my soul

And the company drills
as the gusher spills road kill on highways
Carrion death everywhere
through nights filled with looting

We create a refrain of despair
Glaciers collapse into seawater
Volcanoes erupt with hot ash
The Polar bears are stranded

Yet the pillaging goes on
turning towns to tent villages
There's no safety in building a wall
wetlands are covered in tar balls

Oil slick slides toward the bayous
Destruction and decay slip to disorder
And I greet the terror clinging
to the borders of my soul

En Masse

Traveling incognito
a white-faced mime
unspotted in the crowd
No-one knows his underside
    He's devoid
    of judgment

It's hidden
covered over by
what he says
and what he's spun
    in clothes of
    seething passion

Sometimes his mask slips
Open lipped
he sets truth free
We see a serge of pain
    vanity
    insanity
    emerging

He wanders the world
in our time and place
and we live our lives
side by side en masse
    just so many
    painted mimes

The Shooter

One fine Day

Collegiate
Deviate
Hides in the
pom-poms
an atom bomb

Football
on call It's
all rap talk
sensitivity.
relativity

gun in waiting
down the hall
cares cocooned
Unfair
Unaware

No refuge
from a centrifuge
of anger
insane whispers
of a restive soul hating

Shooter on a rampage
No place to hide
nowhere to abide
He's inside

A Shooter overtakes
dreams
compressing them
to ash
suppressing life

Gunning down
innocence
in one split
second
of thoughtless force

It's over

Slow Down

Gray skies spill fog and acid rain
The snow packs above normal.
in the chill computers transmit
moment's devastation

Tornadoes wash the waste ashore
pouring ocean onto land
We collaborate and mobilize
and a specie disappears

People come and people go
ignoring murder everywhere
finding pleasure as they play while
a cat sleeps, and a dog sniffs

Some drift and dream that
before machines and magazines
and drones life was simple
slow and clean and fair

But war and death were always there
We stumble on and the planet tilts
while lilies bloom and wilt
Everything predictable is limited

Writer's Query in Winter

I stare blankly at the page
Though my email is full
begging me to do battle with cash
confronting malfeasance and rage

Where is it written that I respond?
I am weary of theories and rhetoric
But questions enter my dreams
and haunt me with pointed fingers

So many people lie dying, or
wandering listless and shaken
I cannot take charge for the world at large
Too many children are hungry

While Madam Defarge knits on and on

Syria's covered in smoke and ash
Gaza flashes and responds with flares
North Korea sets off missiles for power
Can compassion survive in the rubble?

But a man finds a purse and returns it
A stranger cleans blood from a soldier's wound
Maybe we are part of an energy plan
that is grand and synergistic

Tulips still break through cold earth

Life Cycle

The mustard grass gold
embroiders spring to summer
altering crops, altering lives.

All seems to thrive in the valley.

There's an echo in spring
when turkeys strut and
feathers spread in mating call.

Apples blossom to fruit
above trailing chicks with scratchy feet
and sounds of whistles and cackles.

Cool Mornings mist about
the new foals and cows moo
to the young in the fields.

Summer fades and the hills
redress in red, brown and yellow
braiding the vista in plaid.

Vine twisted: arms akimbo
clinging to wire
fire-lining the wine fields

Observations

Ambulance sirens mix
sharps and flats
to accompany whippoorwill drumming.

And the old folks watch and
the young folks chase.
Passions burn and burn out in the valley.

So, the old folks marvel and nod
at how everything moves and
another page turns in the valley.

Plants, mountain cats – beehives
bats all of that thrives:
All of that lives in the valley.

Everything pauses in winter to rest
while a new order comes
and the old order ends;

Life cycles again in the valley.

Spirit Dance

A Torah scribed
on midnight blue
space laced on linen

between the laws
embroidered doubts
sewed by daily challenge

Flawed humans rebel
redact and rail against
pronouncements

Windstorms rage
in human souls
yearning for affirmation

But now and then
they glimpse the stars and sense
the arabesque of movement

Beyond the mosque
Beyond the church
Beyond the temples and the chants

All dance as one in spirit

Acknowledgments

A special thanks to Kathy Hainke for her lovely drawings and Waights Taylor Jr. for his publishing know how.

I also want to acknowledge my extraordinary companions and fellow writers who have taken this journey with me. Thank you Scribe Tribe writers Tonya Ward Singer, Arleen Mandell, Jan Cusic, Hazel Whiteoak, and Stephanie Moore, and Friday writers Flora Lee Gantzler, Kathleen Beirne, Margo van Veen, Anita Rowell, Gerry Bearg, Jane Rinaldi, Margery van Dorp. Margaret Raymond and Barbara Shilo's patience, insights, and editorial input were invaluable.

Their encouragement and feedback helped me bring *Pan: the Trickster* into being.

About the Poet

Writing has been the underpinning theme of Maryann Schacht's life and career in social work and psychotherapy. She has always used drama, poetry, and guided imagery to help clients resolve their social and psychological issues.

For five years, she wrote the "Dear Maryann" advice column in the *Jewish World Press*, Albany NY. She was a contributing writer to *OF WESTCHESTER Magazine* in New York. Her work has also appeared in *Jack and Jill* and numerous non-profit newsletters.

She now lives in Santa Rosa, CA, and since retirement her work has appeared in *Tiny Lights*, *Poets of the Vineyards*, and the Sitting Room's annual anthology, and a Healdsburg Literary Guild publication.

Maryann's book *A Caregiver's Challenge: Living Loving Letting Go* is currently on library shelves and in healthcare facilities nationwide. The book was a semifinalist for an award from the Independent Book Publishers Assocation in 1995.

Pan: the Trickster is her first collection of poetry.

CPSIA information can be obtained at www.ICGtesting.com
Printed in the USA
LVOW06s0816080114

368430LV00003B/5/P